# START PLAYING KEYBOARD

## OMNIBUS EDITION: BOOKS 1 & 2

*by Peter Lavender*

**Wise Publications**
London/New York/Sydney

Exclusive Distributors:
**Music Sales Limited**
8/9 Frith Street, London W1V 5TZ, England
**Music Sales Pty. Limited**
120, Rothschild Avenue, Rosebery, N.S.W. 2018, Australia.

This book © Copyright 1984 & 1987 by Wise Publications
ISBN. 0.7119.1283.1
Order No. AM67588

Arranged and compiled by Peter Lavender.
Music processed by Hillmob Music Services.

Music Sales complete catalogue lists thousands of titles and is free
from your local music book shop, or direct from Music Sales Limited.
Please send £1.50 for postage to Music Sales Limited, 8/9 Frith Street, London W1V 5TZ.

Printed and bound in Great Britain by
Caligraving Limited Thetford Norfolk

# Part 1

Keyboard music basics, and the easy-to-read
SFX 'letter-note' music system

# Part 2

Fingered chord technique. Easy transition from
SFX 'letter-note' to standard music notation

# SFX – SOUNDS 'n' EFFECTS PART 1

## About This Book

Welcome to SFX music.

When you play music the SFX way, you become a performing musician almost from the word 'go'. That's because SFX music is easy to read . . . quick to learn . . . and fun to play. What's more, there are SFX music books to suit all tastes and for all occasions.

Before you start, here are a few tips which you will find useful:

Always use the right sound, the right rhythm and the right tempo. The choice of these settings depends on the particular tune you are playing. For instance, you wouldn't put a 'brassy' sound suitable for a march with a gentle waltz. So whenever you play a song, always decide on registrations which fit. A change in the tempo of the rhythm changes the character of a piece of music. Always keep the tempo down to a reasonable speed until you've mastered the melody. And never play a background effect so loud that it over-rides the melody.

Follow the suggested registrations in this book along with rhythm and tempo settings. They are a starting guide while you learn and enjoy playing SFX music.

Finally, get to know all the Sounds 'n' Effects on your keyboard. Explore these exciting features from the start. Vary the sounds and rhythms every time you play the tunes through.

Have Fun.

PL

**All keyboard instruments** have the same layout of black and white keys.

**The black keys** are arranged in alternate groups of 2 and 3 notes:

**A melody** played on the keyboard is a sequence of musical tones. Each of these tones can be written as **music notes** on and around the **staff**.

**The staff** (or "Stave" as it is sometimes called) has 5 **lines** and 4 **spaces**.

**A treble clef** sign is placed at the beginning of the first staff in all SFX music to indicate that the notes are for right hand melody playing:

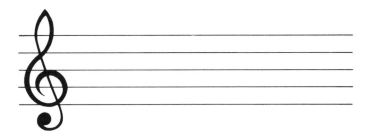

**Each line and space** has a letter name by which music notes appearing in the staff are identified.

To help you to play your favourite tunes straight away, all music notes in SFX songbooks show their letter names.

This makes SFX music as simple as

**In music** the first seven letters of the alphabet are used, and this is how they appear in SFX notes:

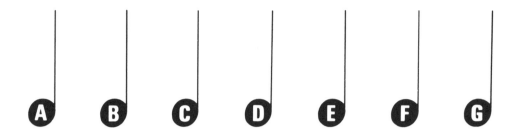

**In SFX songbooks**, most of the tunes use notes from **middle C** upwards on your keyboard.

**Middle C** is in the centre area of the keyboard, immediately left of **two black keys**:

**The middle C note** is written just below the staff. A short line (called a Ledger Line) cuts through the note head.

**The first** 5 right hand melody notes, starting from Middle C, go **up** the keyboard and **up** the staff.

Position your right hand just above the keyboard, with a slight downward curve of the fingers. Starting with the thumb (finger number 1), play Middle C. Release the key then play the next note D (finger 2), release, and on to E (finger 3), F (finger 4), and lastly G with the 5th finger.

Repeat this several times to get the feel of the keys. Try to keep your eyes on each note of music in the staff as you play its key.

Now reverse the sequence. Starting on G (5th finger), play each note in turn, back down to Middle C.

Finally, play all five notes **up** and then back **down** again. Important playing 'pointers': keep your eyes on the music, don't let your hand sag at the wrist, and play all the notes evenly with an equal sounding time for each tone.

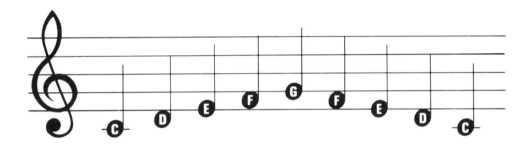

**Music notes.** There are three main types of music notes, each having a *time value* that is counted in regular **beats**:

The WHOLE NOTE  =  ⦿  =  4 BEATS

The HALF NOTE  =  ♩  =  2 BEATS

The QUARTER NOTE  =  ♩  =  1 BEAT

**Bar lines** are vertical lines that appear throughout the staff. The distance between two bar lines is called a **measure**. Each measure contains a fixed number of beats depending on the type of music. A double bar line is always placed at the end of a piece of music:

**The time signature** always appears at the beginning of the music. It tells you the number of beats in each measure, and the type of note that will represent one beat.

The top number in the time signature shows the amount of beats in each measure.

The bottom number indicates the type of note that will have *one* beat. In this "Four-four" time signature, the lower 4 represents the *Quarter Note*.

All other types of notes that occur in the "Four-four" time will be governed by the Quarter Note time value of one beat:

Some well known tunes can now be played on your keyboard using the notes learned so far.

Play the first five melodies with your *right hand only*, using the fingering marked alongside the notes. Take care to give each note its correct time value — the beat count is given in the first few measures.

When you have become familiar with playing these tunes with the right hand, the *left hand accompaniment* can be added.

The following letters appear above the music staff:

These are the names of **chords**. A chord is several musical tones sounding together, providing accompaniment to the melody. By simply playing the appropriate key in the chord section of the keyboard with your left hand, the instrument will automatically produce this accompaniment.

Your Owner's Manual will fully explain the automatic chord function and other similar features programmed into the keyboard.

# Au Clair De La Lune

Traditional

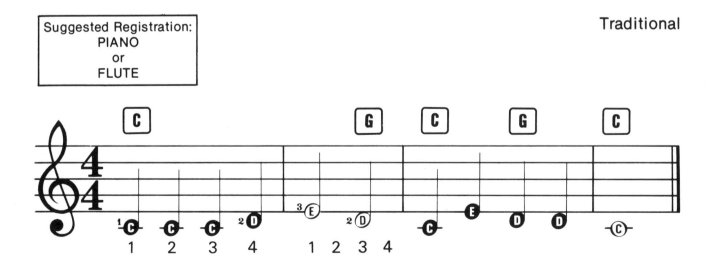

# Largo

by Antonin Dvorak

# Merrily We Roll Along

Traditional

Mer - ri - ly We Roll A - long, roll a - long, roll a - long,

Mer - ri - ly We Roll A - long, o'er the deep blue sea.

The next song introduces the "7th" type of chord: $\boxed{G}\,7$

When using automatic chord accompaniment, your Owner's Manual will explain the simple two-finger left hand key position that produces 7th chords.

If the 7th chord is not programmed into your keyboard, disregard the figure 7 appearing outside the chord symbol box — the basic chord will provide adequate accompaniment to the melody.

# Lightly Row

Traditional

Suggested Registration:
FLUTE
or
PIANO

Light - ly Row, Light - ly Row, on the wat - ers Light - ly Row.

Light - ly Row, Light - ly Row, O'er the deep blue sea.

Gen - tle bree - zes whis - per low, while the shad - ows come and go.

Light - ly Row, Light - ly Row, O'er the deep blue sea.

# Jingle Bells

Traditional

Suggested Registration:
**VIBRAPHONE**
or
**CHIMES**

When you have played these tunes through with chord accompaniment, try adding **rhythm**. Your Owner's Manual will explain this feature.

Set the *Tempo* at **medium** speed, with **swing**, **soft rock**, or similar 'four-to-the-measure' pattern.

**Waltz time** is often referred to as "three-four time", as can be seen from the popular waltz time signature:

This time signature indicates there are 3 Quarter Notes, each with a beat, in every measure:

**The Dotted Half Note.** When a dot is placed after a note, the *time value* of that note is increased by one-half of its value. The Dotted Half Note therefore has a count of 3 beats:

**The Tie** is a curved line that links consecutive notes on the same line or in the same space of the staff. When a tie appears in the music, play the first note and sustain the sound for the full time value of the tied note sequence:

# Barcarolle

by Jacques Offenbach

**Pick Up Notes** occur when a piece of music starts with one or several notes that do not total a full measure. They are played at their usual time value. In most cases the last measure of music rounds everything off by supplying the missing beat. A double bar line usually follows Pick Up Notes.

The words NO CHORD sometimes appear above Pick Up Notes indicating they are best played without accompaniment. This is when the RHYTHM "SYNCHRO" feature on your keyboard can be used most effectively. The Pick Up Notes are played without rhythm, and the "Synchro" feature will start the rhythm immediately you add the chord accompaniment.

The old jazz favourite "When The Saints Go Marching In" begins with three Quarter Notes in 4/4 time signature.

# When The Saints Go Marching In

Traditional

**The next songs** introduce three new notes in the music staff — A, B and C:

By using the fingering marked alongside music notes in these songs, your right hand melody playing will develop a smooth and confident playing style.

# Michael Row The Boat Ashore

Traditional

| Suggested Registration: BRASS or PIANO | Rhythm: SWING or ROCK | Tempo: MEDIUM |

lend a help - ing hand, Hal - le - lu - jah.

# She Wore A Yellow Ribbon

Traditional

| Suggested Registration: GUITAR or TRUMPET | Rhythm: SWING or MARCH | Tempo: MEDIUM |

'Round her neck, She Wore A Yel - low
Rib - bon, She wore it in the spring - time, And
in the month of May And if you
asked her why the heck she wore it, She
says "It's for my lov - er who is far far a - way."

**Repeat signs** are often used in a song when a part or sometimes all of the melody is to be played through again. They save space and unnecessary turning of pages:

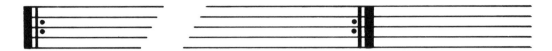

All music appearing between the Repeat Signs is to be replayed.

The word **fine** in the last measure of this song means 'End' — the point to finish playing after the Repeat has been made.

# On Top Of Old Smoky

Traditional

Quite often there will only be one Repeat Sign that appears at the end of a section of music. The repeat is then made from the very beginning:

# Chopsticks

Traditional

| Suggested Registration: XYLOPHONE or PIANO | Rhythm: WALTZ | Tempo: FAST |

**Double Endings**. Sometimes a change in the melody will occur for one or several measures towards the end of a repeat section of music. Double Endings, using 1st and 2nd time brackets above the staff, mark off where a short 'skip' is to be made after the repeat has been played through:

# Wooden Heart

Words & Music by
Fred Wise, Ben Weisman,
Kay Twomey & Berthold Kaempfert

| Suggested Registration: PIANO or VIBRAPHONE | Rhythm: SWING or SOFT ROCK | Tempo: MEDIUM |
| --- | --- | --- |

Can't you see I love you, Please don't
you I say "Good - bye", Then I

break my heart in two, That's not hard to
know that I would cry, May - be I would

do, 'Cause I don't have a Wood - en Heart.
die, 'Cause I don't have a

And if Wood - en Heart.

There's no strings up - on this love of

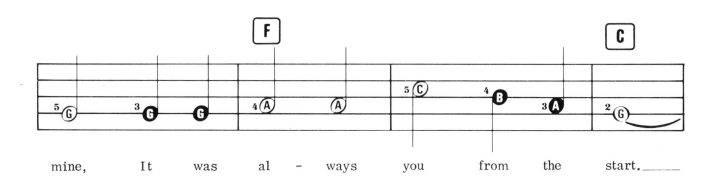

mine, It was al - ways you from the start.____

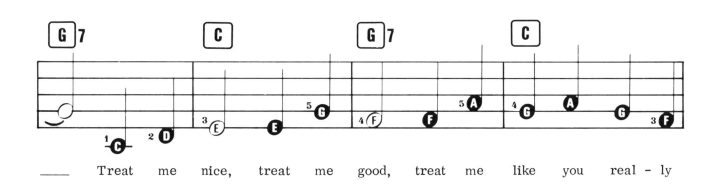

____ Treat me nice, treat me good, treat me like you real - ly

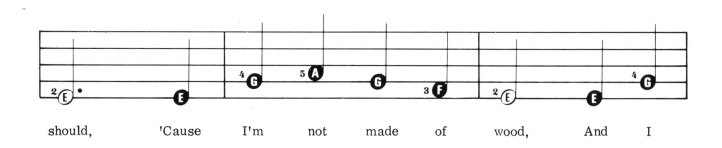

should, 'Cause I'm not made of wood, And I

don't have a Wood - en Heart._____

The "Can Can" has a series of notes running down in the 7th and 8th measures. Try to get a smooth cross-fingering between the notes F and E in the 8th measure.

# The Can Can

by Jacques Offenbach

| Suggested Registration: BRASS or VIBRAPHONE | Rhythm: SWING or ROCK | Tempo: MEDIUM FAST |
| --- | --- | --- |

**Five new notes** continue up the staff, with a ledger line for the last note:

# She'll Be Coming 'Round The Mountain

Traditional

# Where Have All The Flowers Gone

Words & Music by
Pete Seeger

This song introduces a new chord: **D**7

# Love Me Tender

Words & Music by
Elvis Presley & Vera Matson

| Suggested Registration: VIBRAPHONE or GUITAR | Rhythm: SOFT ROCK | Tempo: MEDIUM |

# Snow Waltz

Traditional

# Everyone's Gone To The Moon

Words & Music by
Jonathan King

**The Eighth Note** has a tail:

In pairs, and groups of 4, the tails become *beams*:

The Eighth Note has a time value that is one-half of a Quarter Note. A pair of Eighth Notes therefore equal one Quarter Note:

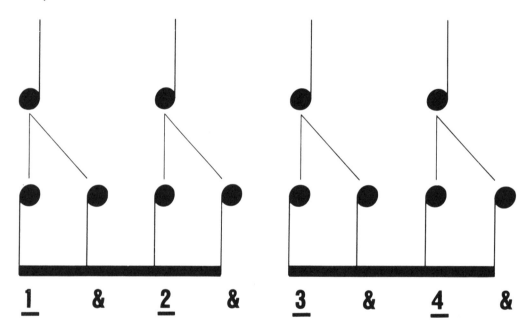

1 & 2 & 3 & 4 &

The "&" used in the Eighth Note count is one way to split the Quarter Note beat.

Another method is to tap your foot in time to the beat. Each down-and-up movement of the toe is a pair of Eighth Notes forming 1 beat.

# Skip To My Lou

Traditional

# Birdie Song/Birdie Dance

Words & Music by
Werner Thomas & Terry Rendall

**The Dotted Quarter Note.**
When a dot appears after the
Quarter Note, its value is
increased by one half:

= 1 beat, + "½ for the dot"
= 1½ **beats.**

The Dotted Quarter Note is
usually followed by an Eighth
Note to make a full two-beat
phrase:

# Silent Night

New chord: **C** 7

Words & Music by
Joseph Mohr & Franz Gruber

Suggested Registration:
STRINGS
or
FLUTE

Rhythm:
WALTZ

Tempo:
MEDIUM

Si – lent Night, Ho – ly night.

All is calm, All is bright. ' Round yon

Vir – gin and _____ her child, Ho – ly in – fant so

ten – der and mild. Sleep in hea – ven – ly peace._____

_____ Sleep _____ in hea – ven – ly peace._____

**Rests**. All our music so far has been a variety of different sounding notes, with a mixture of note values to give rhythm to the flow of musical sounds.

There are moments in all kinds of music however, when a complete silence is briefly needed. These rests are also handy for the casual fingering or "sound" change!

Rests are musical symbols that are written in the staff, and like music notes, each rest has a time value:

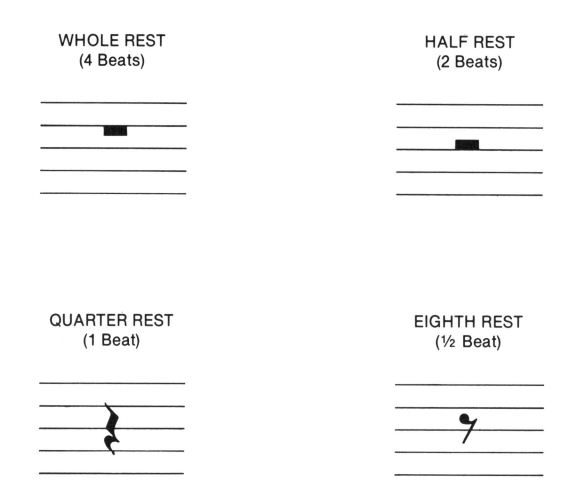

WHOLE REST
(4 Beats)

HALF REST
(2 Beats)

QUARTER REST
(1 Beat)

EIGHTH REST
(½ Beat)

# Gonna Build A Mountain

Words & Music by
Leslie Bricusse & Anthony Newley

**Minor Chords.** The next song introduces the *Minor* chords:

When using automatic chord accompaniment, your Keyboard Owner's Manual will explain the simple two-finger key position in the left hand that produces Minor chord accompaniment.

# Sailing

Words & Music by
Gavin Sutherland

**Sharps and flats.** By the occasional use of the black notes on your keyboard, SFX music now opens up the way for you to play all the great songs in the SFX music books.

This music symbol is the **sharp**:

When it appears just before a note, simply play the *black key* that lies immediately to the *right* of the white key.

This has the effect of **sharp**ening the musical pitch of the written note:

The next song introduces three new chords:

# I Left My Heart In San Francisco

Words by Douglas Cross
Music by George Cory

fog        may  chill   the   air,   I   don't  care!   My   love   waits

there,       in   San   Fran - cis - co,    A - bove  the

blue      and  wind - y   sea.    When   I   come

home    to   you,   San   Fran - cis - co,    your   gold - en

sun        will    shine    for    me.

New chords:

# Annie's Song

Words & Music by John Denver

This is the music symbol called the **flat**:

A flat placed before a note tells you to play the *black key* lying immediately to the **left** of the *white key*. This time, the musical pitch becomes **flat**tened:

New chords:

# Georgia On My Mind

Words by Stuart Gorrell
Music by Hoagy Carmichael

pines._____ Oth – er arms reach out to me,

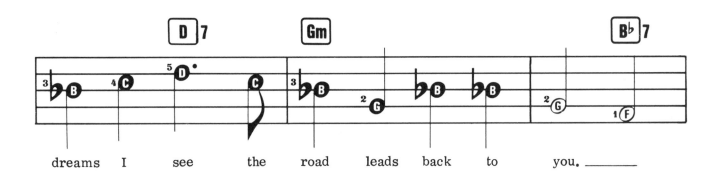

Oth – er eyes smile ten – der – ly, Still in peace – ful

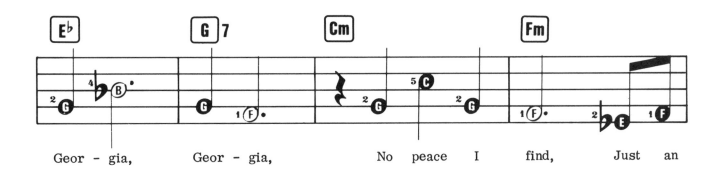

dreams I see the road leads back to you.\_\_\_\_\_

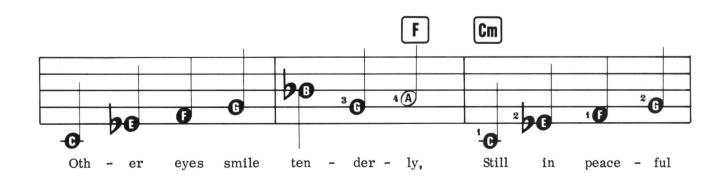

Geor – gia, Geor – gia, No peace I find, Just an

old sweet song keeps Geor – gia On My Mind.\_\_\_\_\_

Sometimes, a tune will contain both sharps and flats:

# Melody Of Love

Music by H. Engelmann

**The Triplet**. This is a group of *three notes* that are all played in the same amount of time as *two notes* of the same value.

The triplet has a small figure 3 placed either above or below the note group:

QUARTER
NOTE
TRIPLETS
$\quad$ = $\quad$ = $\quad$ = **2 beats**

EIGHTH
NOTE
TRIPLETS
$\quad$ = $\quad$ = $\quad$ = **1 beat**

The religious ballad "Amazing Grace" has *Eighth Note Triplets* that contrast effectively with pairs of *Eighth Notes* in other measures:

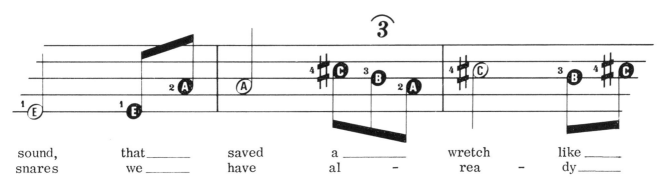

sound, $\quad$ that_____ $\quad$ saved $\quad$ a _____ $\quad$ wretch $\quad$ like _____
snares $\quad$ we_____ $\quad$ have $\quad$ al - $\quad$ rea - $\quad$ dy_____

The words **D.S. al Fine** appear at the end of the music. This means return to the **sign**:—

𝄋

The music is then played through again, and ends at **Fine** in the usual manner.

"Amazing Grace" is an extended arrangement that uses several sharps in the first chorus, followed by a 'lift' in the music pitch for the second chorus. This is known as a **key change**, and flats become a feature of the new key:

# Amazing Grace

Traditional

Suggested Registration:
STRINGS
or
TRUMPET

Rhythm:
WALTZ

Tempo:
MEDIUM

now    I    see.          'Twas    grace    that
lead    us    home.

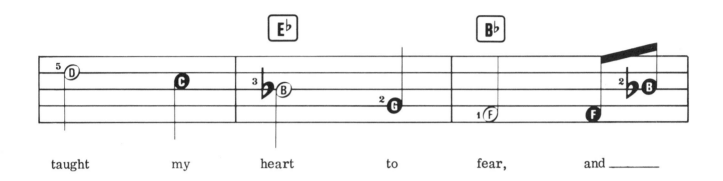

taught    my    heart    to    fear,    and

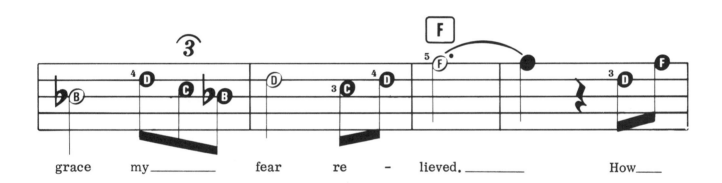

grace    my    fear    re - lieved.    How

pre - cious    did    that    grace    app - ear,    The

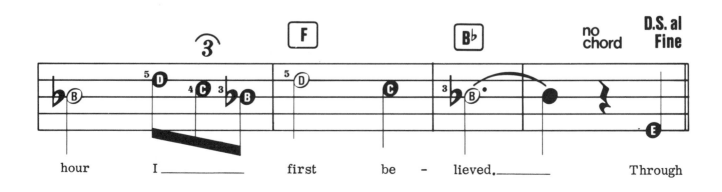

hour    I    first    be - lieved.    Through

**Left Hand Fingered Chords.** Although Part 1 has centered around the automatic features on your keyboard that provide such effective accompaniment to SFX songs, there is an interesting alternative in using *Left Hand Fingered Chords.* Accompaniment for the melody is made with the left hand playing groups of three or four notes – the chords – in the lower section of your keyboard.

If your keyboard can be switched from 'Automatic' to 'Fingered' accompaniment mode, it is recommended that you learn this type of chord playing.

The step-by-step learning and use of fingered chords in Part 2 will open up exciting new ventures into the world of creative music making through SFX publications.

# MASTER CHORD CHART

# SFX – SOUNDS 'n' EFFECTS PART 2

Part 1 of the SFX method showed you how to play popular tunes on your keyboard in a quick and easy way by using the unique SFX letter-note music system and the 'one finger' automatic chord feature.

Part 2 will show you
(1) how to play the professional style 'fingered' chords in your left hand
(2) how to improve and perfect your sight reading and overall playing technique
(3) an easy transition from SFX letter-note music to standard music notation. This is a major step forward in music making that will enable you to play tunes on your keyboard from the immensely popular busker books, and the single note (vocal) lines in everyday sheet music.

Well known melodies have been chosen to help you learn more about music and modern keyboard techniques. Keep exploring all the Sounds 'n' Effects – instrument voices, rhythms, fill ins, tempos, and the add-on effects like vibrato, sustain, reverb, arpeggios, bass accompaniments, sound modulations etc.

Listen to, and play, *all* kinds of music. There are lots of good sounds around!

PL

**'Fingered' Chords.** The one-finger automatic chord feature on your keyboard enables you to play tunes in a quick and easy way, with a variety of accompaniment effects.

To get the maximum enjoyment and musical benefit from your keyboard, it is recommended you also learn to play all the tunes in the SFX method using 'Fingered' chords. Your Owner's Manual will explain how this feature operates on the keyboard.

The first 15 tunes in SFX-Tutor Part 1 use the chords of C, G, G7 and F; finger positions for left hand are illustrated below. Practise these four basic chords, keeping your wrist just above keyboard level and fingers slightly curved onto each of the notes to be played. The fingering numbers are a general guide only, as you may find it easier to use different fingering between more rapid chord changes later.

Left hand (L.H.)

C

G

G7

F

The following 'fingered' chords can be used to play the remaining tunes in
SFX-Tutor Part 1.

The well known tunes you are about to play will introduce new 'fingered' chords. Learn
them, and you will soon be familiar with their sequences in popular music.

A useful 3-point practice routine: (1) play the melody on its own with the right hand,
(2) repeat several times using the 'one finger' automatic chord accompaniment, and
finally (3) play the song using 'fingered' chords.

By following this routine, and using the variety of Sounds 'n' Effects on your keyboard,
you will become a competent and creative player.

**The Quarter Note Triplet:**

Quarter note triplets are very popular in slow ballads. This song from The Pyjama Game makes effective use of these 'laid back' phrases.

New chords:

# Hey There

Words & Music by
Richard Adler & Jerry Ross

Hey There, You on that high fly - ing cloud,

Though she won't throw a crumb to you, You

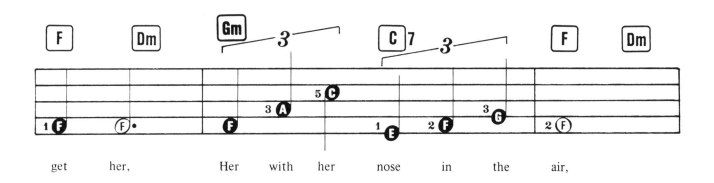

think some day she'll come to you._____ Bet - ter for-

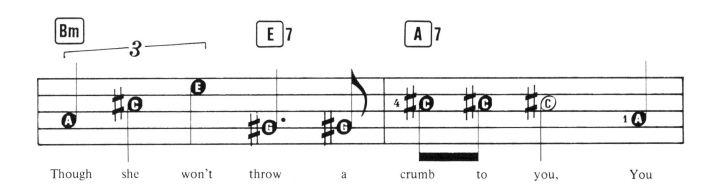

get her, Her with her nose in the air,

She has you danc - ing on a string, Break it and she won't

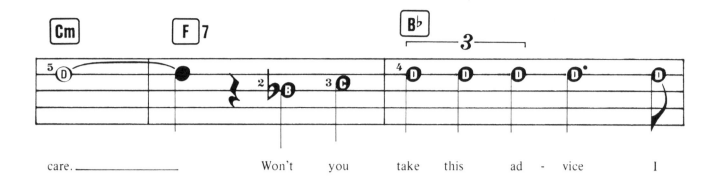

care._____ Won't you take this ad - vice I

give you like a broth - er?_____ Or are you

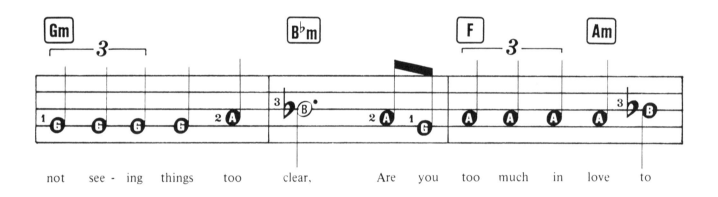

not see - ing things too clear, Are you too much in love to

hear, Is it all go - ing in one

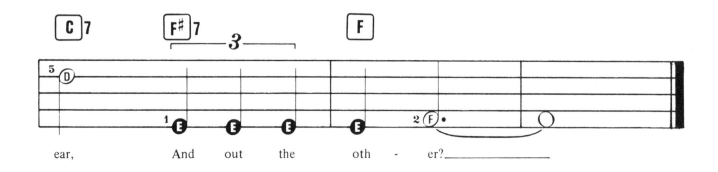

ear, And out the oth - er?_____

The next song has two separate Repeat sections. The latter (pages 10-11) has a combined 1st and 2nd time bracket, with the 3rd time bracket providing the final chord and melody note.

# Feelings
## (Dime)

English Words & Music by Morris Albert
Spanish Lyric by Thomas Fundora

Feel - ings, _____ Noth - ing more than
Tear - drop, _____ Roll - ing down on

Feel - ings, _____ Try - ing to for - get my
my face, _____ Try - ing to for - get my

Feel - ings of love. _____
Feel - ings of love. _____

The Sixteenth Note has two tails:

In pairs, and groups of four, the tails become parallel beams:

The Sixteenth Note has a time value that is one-half of an Eighth Note. A pair of Sixteenth Notes therefore equals one Eighth Note:

The following three measures each show how notes of similar value appear in $\frac{4}{4}$ time. Play the sequence through at a steady tempo, following the counting guide below each note.

Sixteenth notes are frequently beamed to dotted eighth notes. This follows the rule that a dot after a note increases its value by one-half:

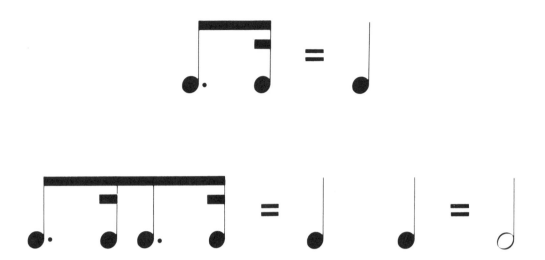

It is the little extra time value, and resulting natural stress on each dotted note, that gives the bouncy 'lilt' to many songs like the ever popular Beatles hit "Yellow Submarine".

# Yellow Submarine

### Words & Music by
### John Lennon & Paul McCartney

Yel - low Sub - ma - rine.    In    the    town _____ where    I    was
sailed _____ up    to    the

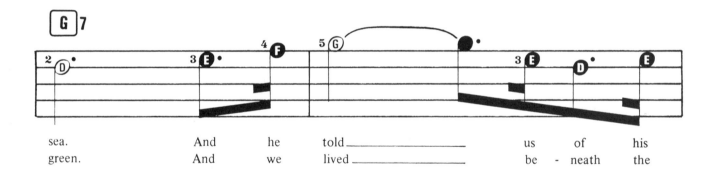

born,        Lived    a    man _____        who    sailed    the
sun,        Till    we    found _____        the    **sea**    of

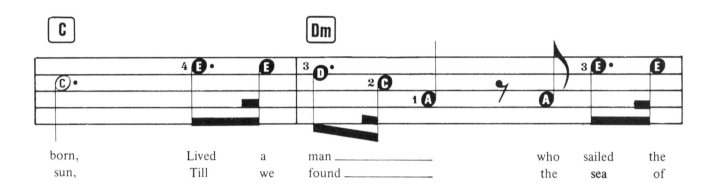

sea.        And    he    told _____        us    of    his
green.        And    we    lived _____        be - neath    the

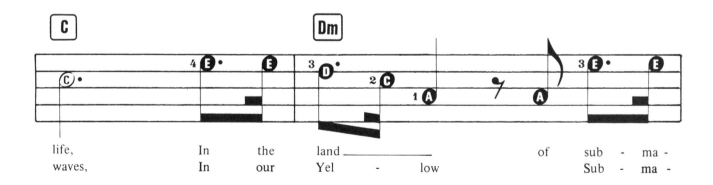

life,        In    the    land _____        of    sub - ma -
waves,        In    our    Yel - low        Sub - ma -

rines.                So    we        rine.

Toreador Song has both eighth note, and dotted eighth note/sixteenth note patterns. Played correctly, these contrasting rhythmic phrases add extra spirit to this famous tune.

# Toreador Song
## (From "Carmen")

By Georges Bizet

The slow ballad "When Sunny Gets Blue" has a variety of sixteenth note figures.

Firstly, the frequently used dotted eighth note/sixteenth note phrase:

The fourth beat of the following measure has the less common reversed form where the first note ("pat-") is quickly followed by the longer sounding second note ("-ter"):

The seventh measure of the song has a pair of sixteenth notes following the dotted quarter note:

Play each of the above song fragments in slow, strict tempo. You will soon get to recognise such phrases and be able to play them correctly in all kinds of music.

New chords:

# When Sunny Gets Blue

Words by Jack Segal
Music by Marvin Fisher

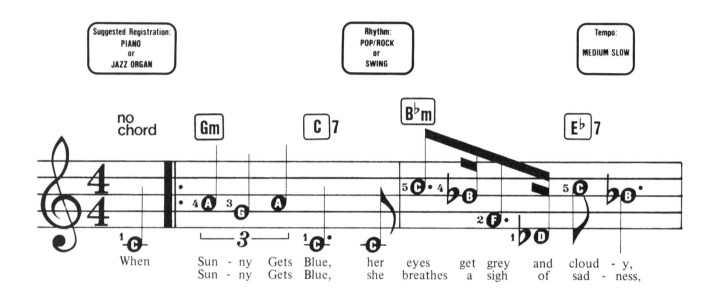

When
Sun - ny Gets Blue, her eyes get grey and cloud - y,
Sun - ny Gets Blue, she breathes a sigh of sad - ness,

Then the rain be - gins to fall. _____
Like the wind that stirs to the trees. _____

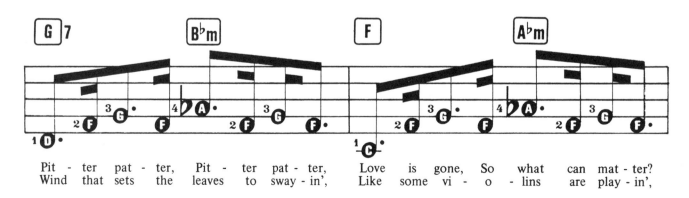

Pit - ter pat - ter, Pit - ter pat - ter, Love is gone, So what can mat - ter?
Wind that sets the leaves to sway - in', Like some vi - o - lins are play - in',

pret - ty dreams will rise up, Where her oth - er dreams fell through,_

_ Hur - ry, new love, Hur - ry here, To

kiss a - way each lone - ly tear, And hold her near When Sun - ny Gets Blue.

Tunes may often go below Middle C, and others extend above top A. Further leger lines are used for these notes.

The next two pieces, "Little April Shower", and "In The Hall Of The Mountain King", use these new notes, and also introduce a musical punctuation sign called the **staccato**.

The staccato is a dot placed over ˙| or under |˙ a note, indicating that it should be shortened and detached from the following note. Its time value remains unchanged.

Drip,    drip,    drop,    Lit - tle

Both tunes have a **Coda**, an Italian word meaning 'tail'. The Coda is a separated section of music that forms the end of an arrangement, and is represented by the sign ⊕ .

Da Capo al Coda, usually abbreviated to **D.C. al Coda**, means return to the very beginning (da capo) of the music, and play through again until you reach the term and sign al Coda ⊕ just above the stave. From this point you make a skip to the Coda and play to the end of the music.

New chords:

# Little April Shower

### Words by Larry Morey
### Music by Frank Churchill

Drip,    drip,    drop,    Lit - tle    A - pril    Show - er,
Drip,    drip,    drop,    Lit - tle    A - pril    Show - er,

66

Beat - ing a tune as you fall all a - round.
Beat - ing a tune ev - 'ry - where that you fall.

Drip, drip, drop, Lit - tle A - pril Show - er,
Drip, drip, drop, Lit - tle A - pril Show - er,

al Coda

What can com - pare with your beau - ti - ful sound.
I'm get - ting wet and I don't care at all.

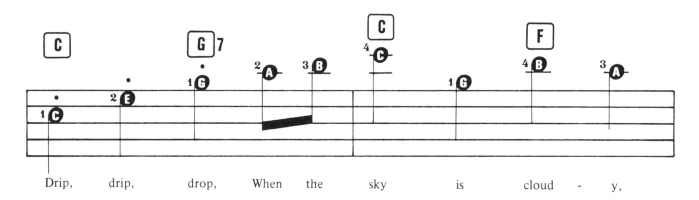

Drip, drip, drop, When the sky is cloud - y,

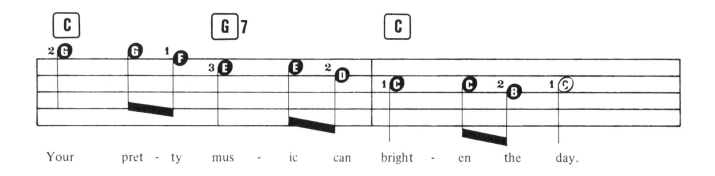

Your pret - ty mus - ic can bright - en the day.

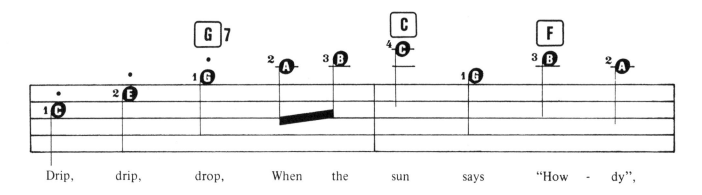

Drip, drip, drop, When the sun says "How - dy",

You say "Good - bye" right a - way. ____

Drip!　Drop!　Drip!　Drop!

I'll nev - er be a - fraid of a

good lit - tle gay lit - tle A - pril ser - e - nade.

Attention to correct fingering is essential in this popular classical tune. Set the Tempo at 'Medium Slow' until you can perform the cross-over fingerings smoothly.

# In The Hall Of The Mountain King
## (From "Peer Gynt")

By Edvard Grieg

A slur is a curved line which spans notes of differing pitch, indicating they are to be played in a smooth unbroken manner:

Do   That   To   Me   One   More ___   Time. ___

In songs, the lyrics often dictate where a slur is required. The word "More" is a blend of two notes, to be sung *and* played smoothly.

A slur will often cover a series of notes, forming a smooth phrase:

Woah, _____   ba -

"Do That To Me One More Time" has **C** for the time signature. This denotes Common Time, and is simply another way of writing $\frac{4}{4}$ time.

# Do That To Me One More Time

### Words & Music by
### Toni Tennille

Kiss _____ me _____ like you just \_\_\_\_ did, \_\_\_\_
Say those words \_\_\_\_\_ like you just \_\_\_\_ did, \_\_\_\_

Oh ba - by, \_\_\_\_ Do that to me once a - gain.
Oh ba - by, \_\_\_\_ Tell it to me once a - gain.

*(Instrumental)*

The automatic features of the modern keyboard can be used effectively at the beginning and during the performance of a song to add variety and character.

The introduction to "We've Only Just Begun" can be played melody only, with no rhythm or chord accompaniment. Rhythm, set at 'Medium Slow', is put on 'Key Start'. The first chord you play following the introduction will start the rhythm accompaniment.

The 'Select' button in the 'Tone Section' is a quick and easy way to change voice registration. The instrument sounds have been paired so that depressing the 'Select' button while playing gives a suitable voice contrast.

An effective ending can be made by turning the Rhythm off where indicated in the penultimate measure and playing the last phrase at a decreasing tempo.

The final measure has a Fermata ⌒ indicating that the last note can be sustained at will.

# We've Only Just Begun

Words by Paul Williams
Music by Roger Nichols

on our way._____
learn to run._____
room to grow._____

Be - fore the ris - ing

And yes, We've just be - gun._____

**CHANGE 'SELECT'**

Shar - ing hor - i - zons that are new to us,

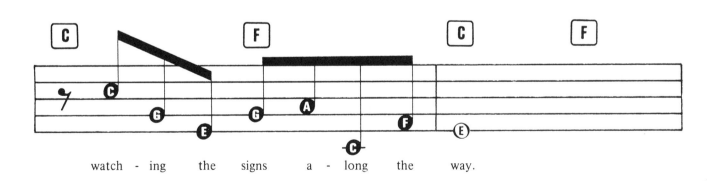

watch - ing the signs a - long the way.

Talk - ing it ov - er just the two of us,

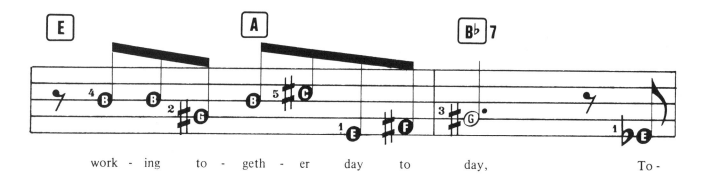

work - ing to - geth - er day to day, To-

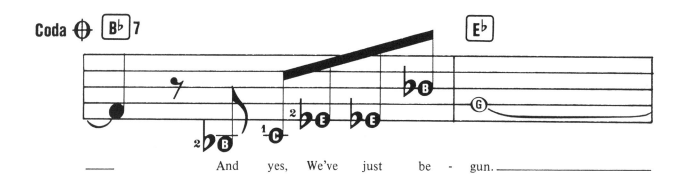

CHANGE 'SELECT'

D.S. al Coda

geth - er, To - geth - er. _____ And when the eve - ning

Coda ⊕ | B♭7 | | E♭ |

_____ And yes, We've just be - gun. _____

| A♭ | | E♭ |

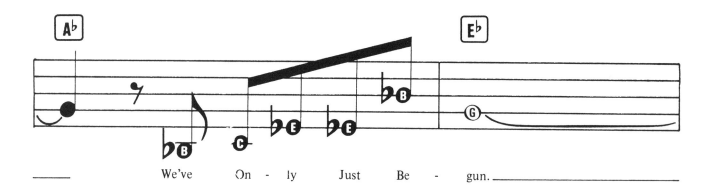

_____ We've On - ly Just Be - gun. _____

| A♭ |  'RHYTHM' OFF | G |

_____ We've On - ly Just Be - gun.

So far your keyboard playing has made good progress using SFX music with its letter-note identification.

'Fingered' chords have extended your playing expertise together with a working knowledge of basic harmony in left hand chord structuring.

You are now ready to play from standard music notation!

This is another major step forward that will provide new creative dimensions to keyboard playing.

Note names for the five lines and four spaces of the staff can be easily remembered by mnemonics:

Every    Good    Boy    Deserves Favours

F        A        C        E

Notes below and above the staff have the same mnemonic:

Go    Away  Big    Cat              Duck    Go    Away  Big    Cat
                                 (below the
                                   line!)

The waltz "Kiss Me Again" by Victor Herbert introduces standard music notation at the 16th measure.

# Kiss Me Again

By Victor Herbert

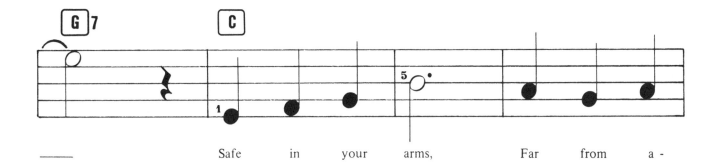

_____ Safe in your arms, Far from a-

larms, Day - light shall come but in vain. _____

_____ Ten - der - ly press'd close to my

breast, Kiss me, Kiss Me A - gain. _____

"Adios Muchachos" is the ideal tune to play in Tango rhythm.

SFX letter-notes are written for the first eight measures, followed by standard music notation for the melodic repeat and finale.

Keep the tempo moderately slow to begin with, and practise up to a lively tango pace.

# Adios Muchachos

## Traditional

Music is often written in Cut Common Time, with the time signature:

This is $\frac{2}{2}$ time, giving a two-to-the-measure feel in the music. Instead of the quarter note representing one beat (as in Common Time, $\frac{4}{4}$), in Cut Common Time the beat becomes a half note. As a result, the music sounds twice as fast as it appears. This is simply illustrated using the lyrics and music of "Ob-La-Di, Ob-La-Da".

In Common Time, with four steady beats to the measure, the song is far too slow:

In Cut Common Time however, with two half notes to the measure and each half note having one beat

the song will flow at a much more lively pace, and the rhythm will feel right:

When playing in Cut Common Time it is best to avoid complex Rhythm and Bass accompaniments in songs with frequent chord changes.

# Ob-La-Di, Ob-La-Da

Words & Music by
John Lennon & Paul McCartney

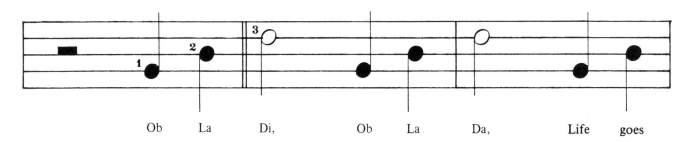

Ob La Di, Ob La Da, Life goes

Bm     Em     G

on,     bra!     La la how the

D7     G

life goes on.     Ob La

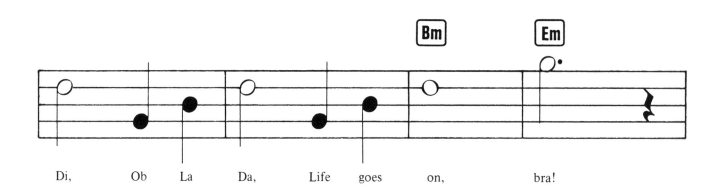

Bm     Em

Di, Ob La Da, Life goes on, bra!

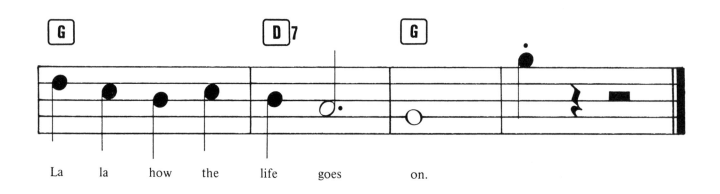

G     D7     G

La la how the life goes on.

Sometimes a song will have a $\frac{2}{4}$ time signature, being two quarter notes to the measure. It is a popular time signature for marches, and lively show tunes like "Diamonds Are A Girl's Best Friend".

# Diamonds Are A Girl's Best Friend

Words by Leo Robin
Music by Jule Styne

**Key Signatures and Accidentals.** A scale is a series of adjacent notes. This is the scale of C:

Only the white notes on your keyboard are used to play the scale of C.

If a scale starts on the note of F, it is necessary to play a B♭ in that scale:

As the note B♭ features throughout the scale of F, a **key signature** can be written at the beginning of the staff:

This is called the key signature of F, and it is then no longer necessary to place a flat sign before the note B in the scale:

The key signature of F indicates that every note B is flattened, irrespective of its position in or around the staff:

The song "Uptown Girl" is in the key of F. A number of notes in the middle section have flats written before them. These are called **accidentals**.

An accidental in a measure will apply to that particular note for the remainder of the measure:

knows___ what she

Subsequent measures are not affected by an accidental; the notes revert back to their basic form:

just   be - cause      I'm   in   love with an

Sometimes a natural sign ♮ may be used as a reminder:

just   be - cause      I'm   in   love with an

A scale starting on the note G requires an F♯:

A key signature of G, with the F♯ as illustrated below, will govern that note throughout the music:

The second song "So Nice", is in the key of G. In the first measure, a natural is used to cancel the F♯. This natural is an accidental, and the key signature's F♯ again takes effect in the subsequent measure:

Some-one to   hold me tight,   that would be ver  -  y   nice,

Remember: accidentals, whether sharps, flats, or naturals, alter the adjacent note and its recurrence within the measure only:

Should it   be   you   and me,   I   could see   it would be       nice.

New chords:

# Uptown Girl

### Words & Music by
### Billy Joel

Suggested Registration:
JAZZ ORGAN
or
GUITAR

Rhythm:
ROCK

Tempo:
MEDIUM SLOW

Up - town Girl, She's been liv - ing in her
Up - town Girl, She's been liv - ing in her

up - town___ world. I bet she nev - er had a
white bread___ world. As long as an - y - one with

back street guy. I bet her ma - ma nev - er
hot street blood can. And now she's look - ing for a

told her___ why. I'm gon - na try for an
down - town___ man, That's what I am.

And when she knows___ what she wants from her

time._____ And when she wakes up and

makes up her mind._____ She'll see I'm

not so tough, Just be - cause I'm in love with an

Oh,_____

_____ Oh._____

_____

# So Nice

Music & original lyrics by
Marcos Valle & Paulo Sergio Valle
English Lyrics by Norman Gimbel

take my hand and sam - ba through life _____ with me.

Some - one to cling to me, Stay with me right _____ or wrong,

Some - one to sing to me some lit - tle sam - ba song.

Some - one to take my heart, Then give his heart _____ to me,

Some - one who's read - y to give love a start _____ with me,

Oh yes, That would be So Nice, _____

Should it be you and me, I could see it would be nice. _____

It is often possible, and very effective, to play two or even three notes together in the right hand to enhance the melody of a song. Such supporting notes to the melody note must be carefully chosen, as they need to relate to the chord being played in your left hand.

# What I Did For Love

Words by Edward Kleban
Music by Marvin Hamlisch

**Augmented and Diminished Chords.** Most keyboards are programmed for 'Fingered' chord accompaniment on the augmented and diminished chord forms.

These distinctive sounding chords are often used in popular music, and have their own symbols.

*Example:*

    C augmented:   C aug, C+

    C diminished:   C dim, C°

The chord shapes are easy to finger and learn on your keyboard.
Recurring patterns of equally spaced notes (intervals) in augmented and diminished chords result in groups of chord symbols having the same note structure:

**Augmented Chords**

C aug = E aug = G♯aug = A♭aug =

C♯aug = D♭aug = F aug = A aug =

D aug = F♯aug = G♭aug = A♯aug = B♭aug =

D♯aug = E♭aug = G aug = B aug =

**Diminished Chords**

C dim = D♯dim = E♭dim = F♯dim = G♭dim = A dim =

C♯dim = D♭dim = E dim = G dim = A♯dim = B♭dim =

D dim = F dim = G♯dim = A♭dim = B dim =

Augmented and diminished chords occasionally have numbers (5, 7,) included in the symbol. For left hand accompaniment purposes, these numbers may be disregarded; simply play the basic chord shape.

# SFX
# MUSIC BOOKS FOR ALL PORTABLE KEYBOARDS

SFX – Designed for musicians or complete beginners.
Build your own SFX library with songbooks for piano, organ,
melody instruments, all electronic keyboards and vocal.

**Start Playing Keyboard 1**
by Peter Lavender
First book in an easy-to-follow course which starts you playing electronic keyboard right away. No knowledge of music needed. Teaches you 28 popular songs.

**Start Playing Keyboard 2**
by Peter Lavender
Play 'fingered' chords with your left hand, improve your sight reading and playing technique. Progress easily from SFX letter-note music to standard notation. 16 popular numbers including 'We've Only Just Begun', 'Yellow Submarine' and 'In The Hall Of The Mountain King'.

**SFX-1: Super Pops**
Seventeen hits including: 'Love Me Tender', 'Annie's Song', 'Tie A Yellow Ribbon'.

**SFX-2: Rock Sounds**
'Jailhouse Rock', ' . . . Blue Suede Shoes', 'All Shook Up', and twelve more big hits.

**SFX-3: Beatles Hits**
Nineteen famous Beatles hits including: 'Can't Buy Me Love', 'Yesterday', 'Hey Jude'.

**SFX-4: Latin Rhythms**
Twenty famous hits including: 'The Girl From Ipanema', 'Quando, Quando, Quando', 'Brazil'.

**SFX-5: 70's and 80's Gold**
Eighteen famous hits including: 'Imagine', 'Just The Way You Are', 'Sing'.

**SFX-6: Country Music**
Twenty famous hits including: 'Don't It Make My Brown Eyes Blue', 'Cotton Jenny', 'Lucille'.

**SFX-7: The Police**
Sixteen of their greatest hits including: 'Roxanne', 'Message In A Bottle', 'Every Breath You Take'.

**SFX-8: Duran Duran**
Fifteen great hits including: 'Rio', 'Planet Earth', 'Union Of The Snake'.

**SFX-9: Easy Favourites**
Twenty-two all-time hits including 'After The Ball', 'Beer Barrel Polka', 'Little Brown Jug'.

**SFX-10: Classical Themes**
Twenty famous themes including: 'Ave Maria', 'Can Can Polka', 'Hallelujah Chorus'.

**SFX-11: Musical Memories**
Twenty hits including: 'Chanson D'Amour', 'Don't Cry For Me Argentina', 'Strangers In The Night'.

**SFX-12: Paul Simon**
Sixteen hits including: 'Bridge Over Troubled Water', 'Cecilia', 'Mrs Robinson', 'The Boxer'.

**SFX-13: Michael Jackson**
Thirteen hits including: 'Beat It', 'Ben', 'One Day In Your Life', 'Thriller'.

**SFX-14: Richard Clayderman**
Fourteen hits including: 'Ballade Pour Adeline', 'L'Enfant et La Mer', 'My Way'.

**SFX-15: Stevie Wonder**
Fifteen hits including: 'For Once In My Life', 'My Cherie Amour', 'You Are The Sunshine Of My Life'.

**SFX-16: Beatles No.2**
Twenty of thier most famous numbers including: 'All My Loving' and 'Paperback Writer'.

**SFX-17: Film & TV Themes**
Seventeen melodies from favourite shows. Includes: 'Edelweiss', 'Fiddler On The Roof'.

**SFX-18: Children's Songs**
Sixteen of today's songs which are great favourites with children. Includes: 'Nellie The Elephant'.

**SFX-19: Christmas Songs**
Nineteen songs and carols both traditional and modern. From 'Silent Night' to 'Mary's Boy Child'.

**SFX-20: Nursery Rhymes**
'Baa Baa Black Sheep', 'Little Jack Horner' - more than 30 songs loved by children everywhere.

**SFX-21: Super Pops 2**
Today's pops – 'EastEnders Theme', 'The Power Of Love' and 9 more favourites.

**SFX-22: Jazz & Blues**
'Bugle Call Rag', 'Satin Doll', 'Take The 'A' Train' - 17 numbers popular with jazz fans.

**SFX-23: Showtunes**
Seventeen numbers from great shows such as 'Cabaret', 'Tell Me On A Sunday' and 'Chorus Line'.

**SFX-24: Walt Disney**
'A Spoonful Of Sugar', 'Bibbidi-Bobbidi-Boo', 'The Bare Necessities' and 19 more Disney favourites.

**SFX-25: Phil Collins**
'Sussudio', 'One More Night', 'Against All Odds' – 13 famous Phil Collins songs.

**SFX-26: Pub Singalong**
Twenty three 'singalong' numbers including: 'Friends and Neighbours' and 'Lambeth Walk'.

**SFX-27: Hooked On Classics**
Twenty four classics arranged in medley form including: 'Greensleeves', 'Swan Lake' and 'The Happy Farmer'.

**SFX-28: Superpops 3**
'Born In The USA', 'Borderline', 'Every Loser Wins' and 'The Lady In Red' – 11 hits.

**SFX-29: TV Themes**
Sixteen popular themes including: 'Bergerac', 'Moonlighting', 'Last Of The Summer Wine', 'EastEnders', and 'Upstairs, Downstairs'.

All these books are available from your local music shop.